GW00391562

Madlynology Poetry

By Madelein De Beer

Acknowledgements

To my pet cat Milo!

Table of Contents

"The Feeling called Love"

The word Love brings to mind
What on earth is this thing we chase?
With all our hearts
But never find if we run after it!

Love is so complex
What if the word Love does not express
The matrix of feelings we feel
The array of sensations it creates

Love comes and goes
Where does it go?
Love for myself
Love for my family
Not loving myself
Or loving myself too much
My ego is massive one minute
And totally deflated the next

It storms like a beast
Knocks you off your feet
It cradles you like a baby
Suffocating you in the making

It lifts you high
Makes you want to fly
It crashes you down

Makes you feel totally lame
Leaves you
Makes you
Brakes you
Builds you up
Fills you with confidence
In seconds
Or leaves you in pain
The same

There is no escaping Love
No matter what form it takes
I would not have it any other way

"Owl"

Owl we need is Love

Owl we are
Is feathers fluffing
Flying and dreaming
Floating and seeing
Specs of Orange and blue
When we Love ourselves
But grounding
Our feet deep
Into the ground
Feeling
Sound

"The Soul's Story"

We are indeed books
Ourselves
With others making the
Mistake
To judge our covers
On the outside
But our image shown
To the world
Is not how we 'read'
And our Soul's story
An untold
Masterpiece

"My inner-child"

A balloon flies high up in the sky
A little boy asks "What's that daddy?"
"It is a balloon flying loose sweetie"

But the little one keeps dreaming
He sees a doggie with a wagging tail

The little boy wonders in awe
What castle the doggie will pause
For a bowl of milk and a fat bone

Dad's attention is drawn to the road
Keeping the little-one safe his main focus

My inner child is starved and hungry
And hiding away in the street

This freedom I seek now and forever more
When I dream stories of happy places
And magical endings, we all long for

I wish with all my heart to set her free
What a gift that would be to me
And to every other human-being

"Balancing Act of energy spent"

When I focus
On the present moment
Spending most of my energy
In the here and now
I don't have time
To play the game
Of yesterday's drama
Or get caught up in
Imaginary gloom
About future doom
That the past and future
Memory spaces
Uses for creation

Sometimes just breathing
And focusing on our
Intention
Benefits
Our hearts more

Yet, it is important
To plan for tomorrow
And solve the issues
Of yesterday
Very much so

Even more important
To never lose sight
Of the bigger picture

And goals you wish to
Accomplish before your
Way too old

The steps
Taken today
This moment
Sees your goals
Manifest
Or never materialize

The thoughts we plant
In this moment
Grows
Whether helpful or not
If you planted thoughts of growth
It could become a tree
Where you can bask in the shade

If you planted nothing
What a shame
Don't wake up
And wonder where
Your life went
When you were not around
It is time to make and create
Every moment count

"Heaven"

Heaven is
Where heart is
Peace

Heaven is
Where the sun
Shines

Heaven is
Where your new born baby
Cries

Heaven heaven heaven
The word and the meaning
Seems intertwined
But heaven is not up there somewhere

Heaven is
Where hearts meets
Lovingly

Heaven is
Where we can stand
Easily

Heaven is
Where we can walk
Effortlessly

Heaven heaven heaven
The word and the meaning
Seems intertwined
But heaven is not up there somewhere

Heaven is
Where humans don't
Have to flee
War and unhappiness

Heaven is
Where the Heart is
At Peace

Heaven is
When the subconscious
Channel is clear
And established

Heaven heaven heaven
The word and the meaning
Seems intertwined
But heaven is not up there somewhere

"The ball"

The ball
Is round
Kicked off
The ground

The ball
Is small
Aimed at
A hole

The ball
Has pressured air
Slammed
With a backhand

The ball
Diamond shaped
Held in hand
For a maul create

The ball
Is plastic
Hit with a stick
Instead of kicked
With feet

The ball
With cork and string
Is bowled
Over two innings

The ball
Is planet earth
Levelling the playing field
In the Universe

"The fine print of our human-ess"

The front and the back
Sometimes do not match
The cover and the inside
Not reflecting true feelings
How easy it is to fool
Those around us
Seeming cool
Playing our roles
With precision
And meaning
Ta-da
We dance
The steps
As we switch between I know
What I am doing
And
I haven't got a clue
Instantaneously
Frowning and smiling broadly
While thinking
I am sinking, I can do this
If you find the switch
Please pass on this very
IImportant piece off
Intelligence
To assist in the decision making process
And understanding
The fine print
Off our human-ness

"Faith in mankind"

We cannot stop, start or rewind
The magical flow of the universe

Lighten up
Feel the warmth
Of your soul
Holding you
Protecting you
Loving you

Allowing you
To let go
Stop trying
To control
Every aspect
Labelling outcomes
As defects
Allowing for
Inner gratefulness
Instead

It's Time
For a new
Feeling to emerge
Our essence
Never seen
Before
Have faith

Mankind
For its time
For us
To shine
Accordingly
To each
Programmed
Set of values

"The yin of the moon the yan of the sun"

My Moon shines yin
Mr. Sun breathes yan
Together they form the
Most perfect dance

My Moon shines light
Soft and cool
Mr. Sun vibrates hot
Hard and warm

My Moon's energy
Inhibited and dark
Mr. Sun's energy
Sexual and bright

My Moon turns crescent
Then half then full
Mr. Sun's happiness
Burns My moon's darkness
Away when the life
Force of Mr. Sun's yan
Warms the entire planet

Mr. Sun's energy so
Predominantly
My Moons energy
Invisible

Bring on rain clouds
Soften Mr. Sun's blow
But don't stop the energy flow
A blessing and a gift to man
Whom baths in the abundance
Off both
My Moon's yin
Mr. Sun's yan

"Projection of essence"

I am human
And you are not
You are a mirror
Reflecting my wounds
That would not exist
If I was not human

Being human
The manifestation
Of a body
An organic
Sculpture
A masterpiece
A piece of art

To be human
Is to only exist
In the now
Tomorrow and yesterday
A place and space
We access
Only through our memory
Never
In the human form

"The Script"

It is time for us
To not just input
And upload
And only be the observer
But be a part and
Play our part
Subjectively
In the script
Written long
Before we were born
The time has come
Even though time
Does not fast forward or rewind
And the chapter playing
Now has played
And will play
Forever more....
The director who
Never calls stop
Projects and Play
With his Stardust awareness
And knowing which
Role he assigns to us all

"Karma"

I see
Because reality
Is not set
In stone
But created
From moment to moment
The variables unknown

The present
The only constant
This clarity and truth
Not totally understood
About reality
Give rise
To twisting
Minds
And truth
When creating
But
Why is one truth
Real and kind
While others
Deemed Hell bound

You blindly
Assume
Abuse your
Imagination
The pure magical
Substance
The flowing current
Within every man
Fret not
Mere mortal man
The Universe is kind
And it is only
A matter of time
Before your lies
Are rectified
Loosening your
Karmic ties

"The power of words"

Words spoken
Into the universe
Words spoken
To others
Forms invisible cords
Verbal agreements
That binds two souls

Like paint on a canvas
Creating streams of colors
Words form concepts
Put's perception into context

Words spoken
Flows with creation
The ebb of feelings
Give it meanings

Words uttered
Wisely into the flow
Does not impose
Expectations or
Break trust
After an agreement
Was formed

It is advised
First to understand
The desired outcome
Before speaking
Seeing we either
Add or subtract
From the meaning

"Anxiety"

What makes
The mind
Send signals
Down the body
Creating
Vibrations
So subtle
That I mind

Jung states
The faculties
Of the mind
Thinking
Feeling
Sensation
And Intuition
And only
One dominates
At a time

Which one
Do we blame for
The anxiety
Created that
I mind
Mind you
Maybe all
Of them
Seeing you think
A thought before
The sensation is
Felt and labelled
As a feeling
By your gut instinct
What if
They are not all mind
Rather separate entities
And needs to work together
To ensure peace
Of mind
And if one part separates
That is the anxiety
You find

"Pictures without feelings"

People visit Places
Pose for Pictures
Post them Publicly
Parading very Proudly
Portraying things Pleasurable

Privately in Person
Playfully and Physical
Personal enjoyed Participation
Plenty and Precise
Present or Past
Periods of Pain
Possibly some Place
Pool or Pond
Paintings and Picnics
People with Passion
Parents and Procreators
Positivity and Pessimism

Planet earth and Plants
Protection and Preservation
Parasitic and Predatory
Passion and Productivity
Pantheism
Peacefully Pause
Patiently capturing the Passage

"Wishes Come True"

Yes you heard me
Wishes Do Come True

There is a sage old phrase
We do not always get what we wish for

I wish to ban this negative code
Into the non -existence mode

Because Wishes Do Come True
And we do get what we wish for

As long as our Heart signal is the same
And aligned to our Mind in the game

Wishing the Best and Biggest for
Everyone that shares the same Stage

"Music"

Music lifts you up
Raises your vibration
From the early days of cave man ravings
Drumming away on make believe drums
We danced to make believe
Dreams we hummed
Until they became real

The current
The flow
The vibration
The energy
The wave
The formless

Music is tapping
Into all the above
Bringing into existence
Pure form
That dynamically
Changes
Depending on the beat
And frequency

The real magic
Of music
Is it transforms

Human Beings
The most
Powerful tool
For creation
In the Universe

"Reading"

Reading in the park
Reading in the bath
Reading the first draft
Reading makes you smart

Reading magazines
Reading short stories
Reading in the mornings
Reading process meanings

Reading in the class
Reading sometimes fast
Reading into a piece of art
Reading stretches the imagination far

Reading with your partner
Reading with your teacher
Reading with your mother
Reading makes you rejoice
In what matters

"Colors"

I see green
And yellow and
Red
I feel soft
And warm
But solid
In my experience
And my view
Only when
Calm
And not challenged

I see blue
And white
And bits
Of brown
When no one
Else is
Around
I feel kind
And balanced
But grounded
In my surroundings

We don't just see
Colors!
We feel them
We actually vibrate
A whole rainbow
A beautiful spectrum
A colorful wave

"Holiday"

Where morning and
Afternoon melts into
Evening
One long dreamy day
Away from home
Families travel far
Some
Drive round
The corner
To escape the mundane
Which is the daily
Routine
Eating ice-cream
Too much sun
Not feeling blue
Late night dancing
Great moves
Then the holiday
Ends
It's back to reality
The daily grind
What you call your life
If fabulous
You don't
Mind
If absolutely dull
You cry
And you sulk
Until next time

"Stones"

We throw them
We grind them
We build with them

We find them
We collect them
We admire them

We look at them
We polish them
We walk all over them

We sit on them
We carry them
We dance around them

We write on them
We treasure them
We take care of them

We believe in them
We hold onto them
We are part of them

We live with them
We grow old with them
We become part of them

We rise with them
We fly with them
We Co-create them
We Art Thou

"Flowers"

Flowers
So delicate
So colorful
So very fragile
So beautiful
So exquisite
When they
Penetrate reality

Flowers
Blooming
Periodically
Where none
Had grown before
How long ago
When the seed fell
The plan and idea
For it to grow
Creating a show

Flowers
Pop up
Suddenly
Breathing
Fresh air "hopefully"
The wind
Caressing their petals
High on mountain tops

Flowers
Drawing you in
Making you notice
Their splendor
In their short existence

Look at me
Look at you

"Summer"

Mr. Sun
Painting
Summer pictures
Delightfully
Divinely
A beautiful sight

As the warmth
Bounces of
His robe
While he dances
Announcing summer
For half
The Globe

"Technology"

Where shall we start?
Technology taken apart
Has enabled
The human race
To become part
Of outer space

How do we find
The balance
The biggest challenge
We NOW need to MIND
Still enjoy the benefits
But at the same time
Take care of the environment
The only way we can breathe full stop!

"Access Space"

To learn is to listen
To learn is to see
To learn is to feel
But pictures and sounds
Are only inputs

The actual processing process
Of sorting like for like
And classifying
Experiences
Before filing them away
Are all inside the Mind

Who knows their own
Filing system?
Tell me how you file
your memories
Is it random or sequential
And how do you access your data?
Object oriented?

Do you know what is already stored
Do you need
More space?
Then archive more!

"Rewriting the code"

Energy
Synergy
Creators
All synonymous

Where the whole
Human-Being System
Is balanced
Aligned to create
To serve
The outcome
Constructive code

Energy
Terrorists
Destructors
All synonymous

Where the whole
Human-Being System
Is out of sync
Not aligned
Cut off from the source code
Death
The outcome
Destructive code

Energy is energy
The Human-Being System programmable
Let's rewrite the code
Without the self-destruct Loop

"The software for Hope"

I dream
You dream
We all dream
Whether we
Like it
Want it
Control it
Or even
Know it

I guess
The key
To Hope
Is understanding
That reality
Is a Dream
That everyone
Can see
Hear
Can smell
Fear

But all the above
Data collectors
Gather only values
And every individual
Has a different experience
Based on the processing in his inner being
And the software
Installed
In his head
That knows hope
And it's meaning

"Communication"

I used to think
I communicated well
Until I experienced
Some discomfort
And the realization hit
Me profoundly
And I thought what
The hell

The words I use
Are the same
In the dictionary
But somehow means
Something different
Entirely

When speaking
To someone
Whose brain
Processing
Is not wired
Quite the
Same as mine

How bizarre
I thought
I laughed
This is shit funny
I communicated
To me
And *only* me

So I breathe
And pay attention
To the setting
And repeat myself
If necessary
Saying the same thing
In a slightly
Different
Processing string

"Evolution"

Ape men
Intelligent design
Some of the results
When evolution itself is queried
Two very different
Thought strings
Are delivered
With different meanings

Develop
Grow
Expand and unfold
You are told
In the results listings
When you google
The meaning
While eating your
Noodles
Which seems to branch
From the ape men
Stance

For the
Intelligent design
To take hold
Further evidence
Of stories as they unfold
Needs first be experienced
Then uploaded
Into Google's immense data truckload
For the results
Are the Human
Experience
Concluded and filed
Into Google's database
Then uploaded
For the crawler
To fetch
And deliver
In your browser
Interface

Printed in Poland
by Amazon Fulfillment
Poland Sp. z o.o., Wrocław

13048644R00023